D0099987

PLANT, COOK, EAT!

A Children's Cookbook

Published by Charlesbridge
85 Main Street
Watertown, MA 02472
(617) 926-0329
www.charlesbridge.com

First published in Great Britain in 2016 by Wayland

Library of Congress Cataloging-in-Publication Data
Names: Archer, Joe, author. | Craig, Caroline, author.
Title: Plant, cook, eat! : a children's cookbook / by Joe Archer & Caroline Craig.
Description: First US edition. | Watertown, MA : Charlesbridge Publishing, Inc.,
[2018] | Includes index.
Identifiers: LCCN 2017012876 (print) | LCCN 2017017832 (ebook) |
ISBN 9781632896896 (ebook) | ISBN 9781632896902
(ebook pdf) | ISBN 9781580898171 (reinforced for library use)
Subjects: LCSH: Cooking (Vegetables)—Juvenile literature.
| Vegetable gardening—Juvenile literature. | LCGFT:
Cookbooks.
Classification: LCC TX801 (ebook) | LCC TX801 .A73 2018
(print) | DDC 641.6/5—dc23
LC record available at https://lccn.loc.gov/2017012876

Printed in China
(hc) 10 9 8 7 6 5 4 3 2 1

Display type set in Aunt Mildred by Akemi Aoki/MvB
  Design, Blue Century by T26, and Lunchbox Slab by Kimmy Design
Text type set in Palatino by Adobe Systems Incorporated
Printed by WKT Company Ltd. in Shenzhen, Guangdong, China
Production supervision by Brian G. Walker

PLANT, COOK, EAT!

A Children's Cookbook

Joe Archer and Caroline Craig

Charlesbridge

Contents

31

42

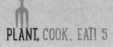

Introduction

Growing your own food is great fun. It's fascinating to watch the tiny seeds that you have sown turn into delicious fruits and vegetables. After weeks of weeding and watering, you will be proud of your tasty home-grown produce.

Get Planting, Get Cooking

In this book you'll find out about how plants grow, and you can follow instructions for how to grow a range of vegetables. Once you have your crops, follow the recipes for delicious meals, snacks, and desserts. From pesto pasta with a twist to a chocolate cake with a hidden vegetable ingredient, the recipes will show you some of the easy, yummy ways you can use fruits and vegetables in all your meals. But they are just a starting point. Use your imagination to come up with your own recipes.

Your Own Patch

Growing fruits and vegetables doesn't mean that you have to have a large garden. You don't even need to have a garden at all. Walls, balconies, window ledges, and fences are all suitable for growing crops. Just fill some window boxes or hanging baskets. You'll soon have some tasty vegetables to eat. Having a small garden also means you won't need to do so much weeding or watering!

Be sure to check the best times for sowing, planting, and harvesting in your region, because climates vary widely. It's time to get planting, cooking, and eating with your friends and family!

What Parts of a Plant Do We Eat?

Let's think about how many different parts of a plant we eat. What's your favorite vegetable? Can you tell if it's a root, a leaf, or a flower?

Roots

Plant roots come in different shapes and sizes. Some roots are long and get food from the soil to the plant; others are thick and store food and nutrients. Carrots, parsnips, turnips, radishes, and beets are all root vegetables.

Stems

We also eat the stems of many plants, such as asparagus and rhubarb. Although potatoes grow underground, they are actually part of the plant's stem.

Leaves

We eat some plant leaves, such as lettuce, raw. Others, such as cabbage, we usually cook. Leaves such as Swiss chard or spinach can be eaten either raw or cooked.

Flowers

Can you think of any edible flowers? Cauliflower and broccoli are actually tiny flower buds, and when they are left to grow, they turn into small yellow flowers.

Seeds

Seeds are often contained in a case called a pod. Sometimes we eat the seeds from these pods, such as peas. And sometimes we eat the pod *and* the seeds, such as green beans or sugar snap peas.

Fruits

We eat the fruit produced by many plants, such as apples and oranges. But did you know that zucchini, tomatoes, eggplant, and pumpkins are all fruits too? Next time you cut open a piece of fruit, have a look at the seeds inside it. All fruits contain seeds.

Bulbs

We also eat bulbs such as onions and garlic. A bulb is another part of the plant used to store energy. When a bulb is left to grow, it eventually produces leaves and flowers.

The Miracle of a Seed

Seeds are an amazing part of nature that plants produce in many different shapes and sizes. But seeds all have one thing in common: they can grow into a new plant.

Sow the Seed

A seed is a plant ready and waiting. Each one has just the right amount of energy to spring into life. This is important to remember when sowing seeds, because if you sow them too deep, the first leaves won't have enough energy to break through the soil.

Seeds don't need to be in soil to germinate, or begin to grow. Pea seeds can begin to germinate with just water and warmth. Place some pea seeds on a folded wet paper towel and leave them in a warm place. After a couple of days, the seeds will have soaked up the water and begun to germinate.

What Happens When You Plant a Seed?

Give most seeds warmth and water and, after a few days, they will begin to grow. If you plant a seed in soil, a root will sprout and grow down into the soil, branching out in search of water. A shoot will grow up from the seed in search of light. Once it breaks above the surface of the soil, the shoot produces its first small leaves. This process is called germination.

How Do Plants Reproduce?

Plants begin their lives as tiny seeds. When a seed is planted, roots start to grow. Roots take in nutrients and water from the soil and help to hold the plant in place. A shoot grows up through the soil toward the light, producing leaves and flowers.

Sweet Nectar

Many flowers have brightly colored petals that attract insects. When an insect lands on a flower to drink nectar, it becomes covered in pollen from the stamen, the male part of the flower. When this same insect goes to another flower, the pollen from the first flower rubs off the insect and onto the stigma, or female part, of the second flower.

Pollination

When the pollen reaches the stigma, the plant is fertilized, and a tiny fruit or vegetable will begin to grow in place of the flower. This process is called pollination. Pollen can be carried from flower to flower by insects, the wind, or by larger creatures such as birds.

Stigma

Petal

Stamen

Bee-Friendly

Without pollination we wouldn't have any fruits or vegetables at all! To be sure pollination will happen, our gardens must be insect-friendly. Attract insects to your garden by planting flowers alongside your vegetables. Have a look in your garden and see how many bees and insects are flying around.

Can you see the tiny vegetables beginning to grow?

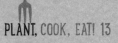

What Do Plants Need to Help Them Grow?

It is very important that our plants get exactly what they need in order to grow. All plants need light, water, nutrients, warmth, and air to grow properly. Let's have a closer look at what each of these does for our plants' growth.

Warmth

Plants need the right temperature in order to thrive—many more plants grow in warm rain forests than in the freezing Arctic! First, seeds need warmth to be able to germinate. Then, once a plant is growing, if it becomes too cold, its tiny cells will crumble and break (test this out by putting some lettuce in the freezer). This is why most of the crops in this book should be planted once the weather has warmed up and there is no longer any danger of frost.

Light

Most of the vegetables in this book require sunshine. This is because plants make their own energy using the power of the sun. Plants absorb the sun's energy through their leaves and, together with carbon dioxide from the air and water from the soil, make plant food from it. This amazing process is known as photosynthesis. A plant without enough light will struggle to grow properly.

Nutrients

Plants get nutrients from soil as well as through photosynthesis, so it is important to ensure that their soil is in good health. We also need these nutrients in our own diets to keep us healthy. We gain some of these nutrients through eating fresh fruits and vegetables.

Water

Plants cannot grow without water, which acts like a transport system that delivers nutrients around the whole plant. When your plants are full of water, they will look strong and healthy. Water helps to keep their leaves and stems stable and upright. If their leaves and stems are weak and floppy, this a sign that they need watering. Many fruits and vegetables also need water to grow to a good size. Apples, pears, and beans, for example, need extra water when their fruits are forming.

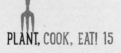

Soil and Compost

The most important part of any garden is the soil. Without it, plants would have nowhere to grow! All soil is slightly different. Some soil contains more clay, making it heavy and thick; clay soil can be difficult to dig but holds on to nutrients well. Sandy and silty soils are much easier to work with but can dry out quickly.

What Is in Soil?

- **Minerals** are released when rocks in the soil break down; they are essential for healthy plants.

- **Water** acts like glue for soil, holding its components together.

- **Air** is present in soil in the form of lots of air pockets, which allow water and oxygen to reach plant roots.

- **Organic material** in soil includes dead and rotting leaves, plants, and wood.

- **Soil creatures:** Soil contains millions and millions of tiny creatures. Some, such as earthworms and beetles, we can see, while others, such as soil bacteria, are so small that we can't see them. All these creatures do an important job by breaking down organic material.

Making Healthy Soil

Healthy soil means healthy plants, healthy vegetables, and therefore a healthy us! To make your soil healthier, it's a good idea to add plenty of garden compost to it. Garden compost is organic material that has rotted and broken down (see pages 18 to 19). Compost gives the soil more nutrients.

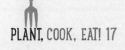

What Is Garden Compost?

Garden compost is a mixture of green and brown plant waste. Green waste is made up of soft green materials, such as vegetable peelings and tea bags, or grass and plant clippings. Brown waste is things like wood chips, cardboard, and leaves. When these combine, together with warmth and moisture, they begin to decompose, which means they break down and turn into compost. Compost can be used to feed plants and soil.

How Does Waste Decompose?

A compost bin is a living world of millions of tiny creatures that turn green and brown material into compost by breaking it down. Worms, ants, and pill bugs, as well as bacteria and fungi, all help to break down the material.

Ready to Use

Compost is ready to use once it has turned dark black and crumbly and you can't recognize any of the material that you put in it. When the weather is warm it can take as little as six weeks from start to finish. The process takes longer when it's colder.

Make Your Own Garden Compost

Try making your own compost pile in an unused part of the garden by creating a pile of green and brown waste from your kitchen and household leftovers. Turn it every six weeks to help the process.

To keep your compost tidy, ask an adult to help you fence it in using wooden pallets. Some cities or towns may supply compost bins. Once you've built your compost pile, watch it shrink as it starts to rot down. Make sure there is plenty of air circulation so that moisture can get in.

You can put almost anything on your compost pile, from tea bags and eggshells to vegetable peelings and grass cuttings. Make sure you also add brown waste, such as scrunched-up paper and cardboard, to create air pockets so bugs can move around in the compost.

Tools and Equipment

Every gardener needs the right tools and equipment to do the job properly. You can do most tasks with your hands, but a few other important tools are needed too.

Digging Fork
A good strong fork is essential for loosening soil and for harvesting crops like onions and potatoes.

Spade
When it comes to digging larger holes and trenches for crops like potatoes, a spade is the best tool.

Garden Hoe
If you sow straight lines of vegetables, you can easily pull a hoe between the rows to remove weeds.

String Line
This can be just a piece of string tied in a straight line to two strong sticks. Although simple, it is an extremely useful tool for growing plants in straight lines.

Hand Trowel and Fork

Trowels are perfect for scooping and lifting small plants into the garden and for making trenches. A hand fork is the best tool for weeding your plot.

Other Useful Equipment

String, scissors, pruning clippers, and a wheelbarrow are all handy to have but are not essential.

Garden Supplies

You may also need netting for protection from birds and bamboo canes for building trellises for bean and pea plants to climb as they grow. You'll need to buy seeds and a bag of multipurpose compost. You might also want to buy new pots and seed trays. There is a list of suggested seed varieties on pages 106 to 107.

If you are going to buy new equipment, it's worth buying good-quality tools so they will last for many years to come.

Preparing Your Vegetable Patch

When the weather starts to warm up, you can choose where you want to have your vegetable patch and what vegetables you want to grow.

Which Spot Should You Choose?

Vegetables like lots of sunshine, so choose an area that isn't shaded by trees or buildings. Watch the sunshine in your garden over the course of a day and look for the sunniest spots. These places will be good locations to grow your vegetables. Use a compass to find out which direction your garden faces. A garden that faces south will generally get the most sunshine.

Making a Vegetable Patch

Remember that the more you take on, the more work there will be! A good size for a small vegetable patch is 5 by 10 feet. This should give you enough space to grow a number of different vegetables. Your patch could be part of an existing flower bed or you could make one from scratch! Why not make a raised bed using timber planks as edges? Get an adult to help secure the planks to wooden posts at each corner.

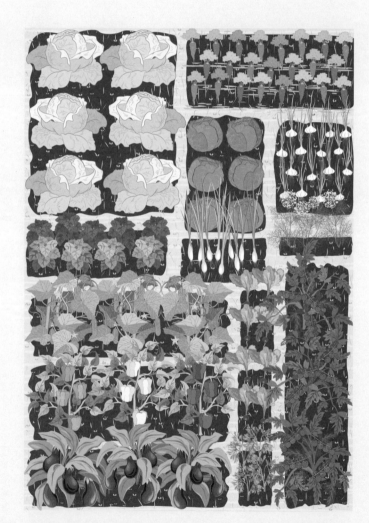

Preparing the Soil

Make sure that the area you choose is free from weeds. Use your hand fork to dig them up. Make sure you remove old roots or they'll keep growing back again.

When the area is clear of weeds, dig over the plot with your fork or spade to break up hard soil so the roots of your vegetables will find it easier to grow. Break up any big clods using the back of the fork.

Finally, use a rake to make sure the top of the soil is fine and crumbly. This will make it much easier to sow seeds and plant seedlings.

Sowing Seeds Indoors

When it is too cold to sow delicate seeds, such as tomatoes and eggplants, outside, you can start to grow plants indoors. This means that you can control how much light, water, and warmth your seedlings get. This will help them grow into big and healthy plants once they are moved outside.

Pots and Seed Trays

For all of the seed sowing in this book, you will need small pots or seed trays. There is a wide range of different pots and seed trays that you can use for sowing your seeds. Pots that are 3 ½ inches in diameter and plug seed trays are ideal for the job.

Yogurt containers, egg cartons, and cardboard tubes make great pots too. Whatever you use, put holes in the bottom for excess water to drain away.

Compost

It's always best to buy suitable compost to grow your seeds in. Multipurpose compost will be free from weed seeds and diseases and will have the right amount of nutrients to feed your plants when they are young.

Where to Grow Them

Greenhouses are usually very warm and therefore an ideal place to grow seedlings. However, using a sunny windowsill can be just as good. Find ones that get plenty of sunshine throughout the day.

How to Sow into Pots

Fill each pot with compost. Level the compost with your hand, then give each pot a few taps on the table to help the compost settle. There should always be a gap of about a half inch at the top for when you water the seedlings. Otherwise water may flow over the top of the pot and could take smaller seeds with it!

Place the required number of seeds on top of the compost. Don't be tempted to sow the whole pack into one pot! Seeds need to have enough space to grow.

Larger seeds can easily be pushed into the compost. Smaller seeds need to be lightly covered with a little more compost. Use another slightly larger pot as a sieve. Put a little compost into the bottom of the spare pot and gently shake it over the top of your seeds until they are covered. Water your pots.

Thinning Out Seedlings in Pots

Once the seeds have germinated, you will have to remove some of the seedlings to make enough space for one plant to grow. This process is called thinning out. Sometimes it is possible to plant the seedlings you've removed in their own pot. If a thinned-out seedling's roots and shoot are intact, make a hole in another pot of compost and drop it in.

Sowing into Plug Trays

1. Cover the whole tray with compost. Make sure every cell is full.

2. Level off the compost with your hand.

3. Use your finger to make a little hole about ¼ inch deep in each cell.

4. Now it's time to sow the seeds. If the seeds are small, such as lettuce or tomatoes, put two or three seeds into each cell.

5. Place larger seeds, such as beans or peas (shown), on the soil and push them in.

6. Cover the seeds with more compost using a larger pot as a sieve.

7. To finish, water your seeds. You must use a watering can with a fine spray that won't drown or wash away your seedlings.

Label pots and trays with the date and the name of what you have sown.

TIP!

To keep your seeds growing straight and strong, turn the trays around every couple of days. Keep pots and trays moist but not soaking wet.

Sowing and Planting Outside

Once the weather has warmed up, seeds can be sown straight into the soil. Check that you can feel warmth in the soil. There should be no overnight frosts, and temperatures should be a minimum of 50°F. If it is too cold, your plants won't grow.

Sowing Seeds Outside

1. Use a string line to mark out where you want to sow your seeds. This helps you to sow in a straight line.

2. Make a shallow trench in which to sow your seeds. The depth of the trench will be different for each crop. You can use a garden hoe, a trowel, or simply your fingers to make the trench. Try to keep it the same depth all the way along.

3. Place your seeds in the trench at the required distance apart. Carefully cover them with soil.

4. Water your seeds and watch them grow!

Thinning Seedlings Outside

It may be necessary to thin your crops. Each vegetable will be different, but all require enough room to grow properly. The closer together they are, the smaller they will be. It may be hard to throw away young seedlings, but if you don't do this, your crops will compete against one another for light and nutrients, and you will end up with fewer, smaller vegetables.

Hardening Off

If you have grown plants from seeds in pots and trays inside, you must first harden them off. It can be quite a shock for young plants to be planted straight outside. To prepare them, introduce them to the outdoors slowly. Place them outside during the day and bring them in at night. Do this for about a week.

Planting Outside

Dig a hole roughly the same size as the root ball of the plant. Place the plant in the hole, fill the soil in around it, and gently pat it firm. Plants are very fragile when they are young, so make sure you don't pile the soil too high up against their stems, because this could cause rotting. Lightly water your plants, and keep them moist during the first few weeks.

Everyday Gardening Tasks

Once your seeds and seedlings are in the ground, a big part of making your vegetable garden a success is looking after it as often as you can. By completing some simple everyday jobs, you will make sure to get the best harvests.

Watering

Your crops will soon let you know if they need water. Their leaves will droop, and the plant will look limp. Most vegetables need watering at least twice a week. When the weather is hot and dry, you'll need to water them every day. Aim to get water to the roots, and keep the soil moist but not soaking wet.

Weeding

Weeds in your vegetable patch will compete with your crops for water, light, and nutrients. Use a hand fork or a hoe to lift out the weeds, including the roots. You'll need to keep on top of this task, as weeds can grow very quickly!

Fertilizer

Sometimes plants need a little help to get all the nutrients they need. Using fertilizer will make sure your plants are as healthy as possible. The easiest and most natural way to use fertilizer is to add well-rotted garden compost and manure to your soil. You can also scatter organic liquid fertilizers or plant food around the base of your crops. Always read the labels on the bottles carefully, and ask an adult to help.

Harvesting

An easy way to tell if your crops are ready to pick is to see whether they are a similar size and color to vegetables you would buy at the store. If they're ready, then it's time to harvest and eat them! Crops such as beets, carrots, and onions are picked only once. Vegetables such as beans, peas, and zucchini will produce many crops. These need to be harvested almost every day during the height of their growth period. Look for crops hiding away underneath leaves, and make sure you pick them before they become too big!

Wildlife in the Garden

Look around your garden and you'll soon see that it's home to many creatures—from tiny ones, such as bumblebees and spiders, to much larger creatures, such as birds and squirrels. Many crops couldn't grow without help from these animals.

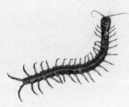

Friends in the Garden

Honeybees, bumblebees, and other insects play a vital role in pollinating many vegetable crops. Therefore it is important that we make our gardens a place they like to visit. Fill your garden with as many bee-friendly plants as possible, such as lavender and buddleia. You could also build places where bees like to live. Why not try making a bee hotel out of old bamboo canes?

Worms are another essential creature. They help to break down garden waste and leaves. Worm dung is the perfect nutrient for a plant to take up through its roots! Worms also make lots of tunnels within the soil. These tunnels allow water and air to reach plant roots.

Ladybugs may look harmless, but they are very good at eating problem pests such as aphids.

Other small creatures such as centipedes, hoverflies, spiders, lacewing larvae, and wasps eat insects that could potentially damage crops. Encourage these creatures wherever possible, and they will keep the number of pests down.

Frogs, toads, and birds love to eat some of the most troublesome pests in the garden such as slugs and snails!

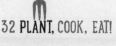

Garden Pests

While there are many creatures that are useful and welcome in the garden, there are others to keep away! Check your plants regularly for damage. If you find any pests, remove them and put them on the compost pile.

Slugs and snails are perhaps the most destructive pests in the garden. They can quickly munch their way through leafy crops, such as lettuce or cabbage. Encourage creatures such as blackbirds, frogs, and toads that like to eat slugs and snails.

Move hungry *caterpillars* to the compost pile. It is worth covering any vegetables in the cabbage family, such as kale, cabbages, or brussels sprouts with fine netting. This will prevent cabbage white butterflies from laying eggs on them.

Rabbits and deer are common pests in rural areas and can destroy all your hard work! The only way to stop this from happening is to make a strong barrier, such as a fence, around your vegetable plot.

Birds can also eat your precious crops. Putting nets over plants can help stop hungry birds.

Protect your small plants by covering them with glass jars or the bottom of plastic bottles.

Aphids are tiny insects that suck the sap—an important nutrient-rich liquid—out of leaves and stems. They usually attack in large numbers. Try to wipe them off where possible, or gently move ladybugs from other plants in the garden to vegetables that have an aphid problem.

Diseases

There are also many plant diseases that can affect harvests. Fungal problems, such as potato or tomato blight, can destroy crops within a few days. You'll recognize blight as dark, rotting patches on the leaves and stems of plants (see picture at right). Unfortunately there is no way to treat the problem. As soon as you notice it, harvest any unaffected vegetables and dig up the infected plant. The fungus can be blown around by wind and splashed by raindrops, and therefore is usually a problem in wet, humid weather.

Powdery mildew (pictured at left) is another fungus that attacks plants and can cause white cloudy patches to appear on leaves. Plants such as peas and zucchini are prone to mildew attack. It can be difficult to prevent, but keep plants well watered and make sure they have enough space to grow properly. Crops planted too close together can be prone to fungal problems. Cut off any badly infected leaves.

Healthy Eating

Diet is an important part of a healthy lifestyle. What you choose to eat can have an enormous impact on your energy and health. This is why it is important to learn how to eat well and make the right choices.

Nutrient-Rich

You can't see most nutrients, but they are in all foods, in varying amounts. Fruits and vegetables, especially home-grown or organic vegetables, are some of the best sources of healthy ingredients.

A Rainbow of Fruits and Veggies

Vegetables and fruits should form a large part of all our diets. Every day, aim to eat a rainbow of different colors, textures, and varieties. The fresher they are, the more goodness there is inside them. Wash raw vegetables and chew them well.

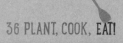

Food Groups

For a balanced diet, aim to eat food from all five main food groups. Each food group contains different nutrients that work together to keep the body healthy. These groups are often shown on a food plate that illustrates the proportions in which they should be eaten.

Fruit and vegetables are full of vitamins and minerals and keep our digestive system healthy.

Carbohydrates such as bread, pasta, and rice provide us with energy.

Protein builds and repairs our bones, muscles, skin, hair, and body tissues. Meat, fish, eggs, and beans contain protein.

Dairy products such as milk, butter, yogurt, and cheese help to build strong bones and teeth.

Fats keep us warm and can be stored in the body for energy. Foods that are high in fats, such as cakes, cookies, and chips, should be eaten only in small amounts. Fats found in oily fish, olives, nuts, and seeds are a healthier alternative.

Get Ready to Cook

Once you've harvested your vegetables, you'll want to start making some tasty dishes. But before you start cooking, there are some important things you need to know.

Be Prepared

Make sure you have the ingredients you need for the recipe. You don't want to get halfway through cooking and discover that you're missing a vital ingredient. Check that you have all the equipment that you need too. Then you're ready to cook!

Oven

Your oven should be preheated to the specified temperature. Always ask an adult to help turn the oven on for you and ask for help when using the stovetop. Use oven mitts when handling hot pans or baking sheets.

Health and Safety Tips

1. Wash your hands with soap and warm water before you start.
2. Tie back long hair.
3. Rinse and dry all fruits and vegetables thoroughly.
4. Read through the recipe twice before you start cooking and check that you have all the equipment and ingredients.
5. Immediately after preparing raw meat, remember to thoroughly clean everything that came in contact with it, such as the cutting board, knife, work surface, and your hands.

Cooking Equipment

Here are the most important tools and appliances for the recipes in this book:

- Oven: for baking and roasting
- Stovetop: for boiling, simmering, and frying
- Blender or food processor: for making purees, soups, and pestos
- Sharp knife: for chopping and slicing
- Cutting board: essential for chopping and slicing on
- Metal spatula: for scraping food off pans and baking sheets and preventing food from sticking to them
- Wooden spoon: for stirring
- Medium, small, and large mixing bowls
- Garlic press

- Masher
- Sieve
- A variety of cooking pans and baking sheets (large, medium, and small saucepans and a large frying pan or wok)
- Casserole dish
- Slotted spoon
- Tongs
- Measuring cups and spoons
- Vegetable peeler
- Cheese grater
- Pastry brush

Of course you'll want an apron too!

LET'S GET STARTED!

Growing Carrots

There is nothing more satisfying than pulling up your own carrots, straight from the soil. Their seeds can be sown in the ground or in deep pots and containers.

Growing Carrots in the Ground

1. First prepare a seedbed using the instructions on page 28.

2. Use a string line to mark out where you want your row. Leave 12 inches between rows.

3. Using a trowel, or your fingers, make a trench a little less than 1 inch deep.

4. Carefully place a row of seeds in the trench, leaving a finger space between each seed.

5. Cover the seeds with soil and water them. Seedlings will appear in two to three weeks.

6. To make sure that each seedling has enough space, thin them as described on page 29. The aim is to give each carrot about 4 inches of space. Keep the strongest seedlings and pull out the others.

7. Your carrots will be ready to harvest in six to eight weeks. Hold their leaves and pull them gently from the soil.

Growing Carrots in Containers

Growing carrots in containers can give better results. Use a container that is at least 8 to 12 inches deep and has holes in the bottom so excess water can drain away. Don't put too many seeds in one pot or the carrots won't have room to grow to full size. Pots dry out very quickly, so check them daily to ensure they're still moist.

Carrot Problems

To make sure you get straight carrots, check that the soil doesn't have any large stones, which can cause carrots to fork. Uneven moisture can cause carrots to crack (see picture at left).

Carrot Scramble

serves
4

2 large sweet potatoes

12 slices bacon

1 large leek, white part only, sliced

Salt and pepper

8 large carrots, peeled and chopped

1 lemon, halved

2 tablespoons butter

Drizzle of olive oil

1. Preheat the oven to 350°F.

2. Bake the sweet potatoes for 45 minutes to an hour, until a fork goes in easily.

3. While the sweet potatoes are baking, cook the bacon in a frying pan until browned. Drain.

4. In a separate frying pan, cook the leek, sprinkled with salt and pepper, for 5 to 10 minutes on medium heat, stirring often, until softened. Chop the bacon and stir it in.

5. Cook the carrots in a pot of boiling salted water for 10 minutes, until tender. Drain them and mash them in a large bowl.

6. When the sweet potatoes are cooked, halve them and scoop out the flesh. Add the sweet potato to the carrot and roughly mash them together. Season with salt and pepper and the juice of half the lemon.

7. Add the butter and olive oil, followed by the bacon and leek mixture. Add the juice from the other half of the lemon if you wish.

Did you know that carrots weren't always orange? In the seventeenth century the most widely grown variety was purple!

Watch out for birds! They could eat all your kale overnight; it may be wise to put some netting around your crop.

Growing Kale

Kale is in the same family as cabbages and broccoli. We eat the leaves of the kale plant, which taste sweeter when harvested after a frost.

Sowing Seeds Indoors

Follow the instructions for sowing into pots or plug trays on pages 26 to 27. Sow two seeds per pot or cell. Once the seeds have germinated, pick out the weaker seedlings, leaving one in each pot or cell. When the plants have reached 8 inches in height and have been hardened off (see page 29), it's time to plant them outside.

Planting Outside

1. Use a hand trowel to dig a small hole in the soil.

2. Place the plant in the hole. Be sure to firmly push the soil back in around the plant.

3. Give each plant plenty of space to grow. About 18 inches between each plant is ideal.

4. Water well in the first few weeks of growth and the plant will grow quickly.

5. Begin to harvest the leaves three to five months after planting. Pick a few small, tender leaves. Leave the smallest leaves at the top. They will be your next harvest.

Kale Pesto Pasta

serves 4

14 ounces dried pasta

10 ounces kale

2 ounces fresh basil, stems discarded

¾ cup pine nuts

½ cup grated Parmesan cheese

1 clove garlic, crushed

4 to 5 tablespoons olive oil

1 to 2 tablespoons Greek yogurt

Juice of 1 lemon

1. Cook the pasta in a large pot of boiling salted water, stirring occasionally, until al dente; drain and return to the pot.

2. Tear the kale leaves into smaller pieces; discard the stems. Cook in a second pot of boiling salted water for 1 minute.

3. Drain the kale, and when it's cool, squeeze out as much water as you can.

4. Pulse the kale, basil, pine nuts, Parmesan, garlic, olive oil, yogurt, and lemon juice in a food processor or blender until smooth.

5. Stir the kale mixture in with the pasta.

6. Serve immediately.

Growing Peas

Peas can be sown in colder temperatures. In about three months, your peas will start to produce pods—inside are peas, the sweetest vegetables in the garden and best eaten right away!

Sowing Seeds

1. Pea seeds can be sown directly into the ground, or you can start them in trays indoors. Follow the indoor sowing instructions on pages 26 to 27. Put one seed in each pot.

2. Place them outside, off the ground or, for faster germination, on a windowsill.

3. Peas germinate and grow quickly. Once you can see the roots growing through the bottom of the pot, it's time to harden them off (see page 29) and plant them outside.

Planting Peas in a Pot

1. Fill a large pot with multipurpose compost (you could use some garden soil first and then top it off with compost).

2. Using four bamboo canes (about 5 feet long), make a small tepee trellis. Get an adult to help tie it together at the top.

3. Plant the pea plants around the edge of the pot. They will need about 6 to 8 inches of space between them.

4. The peas will need something to climb up. Tie some netting or twigs to the trellis.

WATER & WATCH THEM GROW!

5. Watch for the pea flowers. When they fade away, the pea pods will appear and begin to swell. When they're nice and fat, they're ready to pick.

How Do Peas Climb?

Peas have curly stems that cling to structures. These are called tendrils and help the plant climb closer to sunlight.

Pea Gnocchi

One serving of peas contains as much vitamin C as two large apples and more fiber than one slice of whole-wheat bread.

serves 4

1⅔ cups shelled peas

2 cups ricotta cheese

⅓ cup grated Parmesan cheese

1 egg

Salt and pepper

1 cup flour

Drizzle of olive oil

Generous squeeze of lemon juice

A few mint leaves

Zest of ½ lemon

1. Place the peas in a heat-proof bowl and cover them with boiling water to soften them.

2. After a minute, drain the peas, and set 4 tablespoons of them aside in a separate bowl. In a large bowl, mash the remaining peas to a paste using a fork, potato masher, or handheld blender.

3. Add the ricotta, Parmesan, egg, and salt and pepper, and mix well. Then add the flour little by little, stirring slowly.

4. Roll a teaspoon of gnocchi batter into a ball in your hand and place it gently in a pot of boiling water. You can cook about 12 at a time.

5. When the gnocchi float to the surface, they are ready. Fish them out with a slotted spoon and place them in a serving dish.

6. Spoon the peas you set aside earlier into the serving dish. Top with the olive oil and lemon juice. Garnish with the mint leaves, lemon zest, some pepper, and an extra teaspoon of Parmesan.

7. Serve immediately.

Growing Lettuce

Lettuce is quick and simple to grow. Seeds can be sown straight into the soil, but they also grow well in pots and window boxes. Lettuce is crisper and sweeter eaten fresh.

Sowing

1. Place two lettuce seeds in each cell or pot, cover them, and water them. Place on a sunny windowsill.

2. When the seeds have germinated, thin them by removing one seedling from each cell or pot.

3. Be sure to harden off lettuces (see page 29) before you plant them outside.

Planting Outside

1. Your lettuce will be ready for planting outside once you can see the roots growing through the bottom of the pot or tray.

2. Lettuce will grow well in a slightly shaded spot. If it gets too much hot, bright sun, lettuce may "bolt," or produce a flower stalk, which makes the leaves taste bitter.

3. Watch out for slugs, which love to eat lettuce! If this is a problem, grow your lettuce in containers and place them off the ground, or in hanging baskets or window boxes.

4. Lettuce plants will be ready to harvest in about eight to twelve weeks.

Cut and Come Again

Lettuce is known as a "cut and come again" crop because most lettuce leaves can be picked and will grow back time and time again.

Lettuce Scoops

serves 4

3 to 4 heads of little gem or romaine lettuce

4 cans tuna fish, drained

½ small red onion, finely chopped

Handful of fresh cilantro, finely chopped

Handful of cherry tomatoes, quartered

4 tablespoons Greek yogurt

2 tablespoons mayonnaise

2 tablespoons capers

Squeeze of lemon juice

Drizzle of olive oil

Black pepper

1. Separate and wash the lettuce leaves, then carefully dry them in a clean towel or salad spinner.

2. Place the tuna, red onion, cilantro, cherry tomatoes, yogurt, mayonnaise, capers, lemon juice, and olive oil in a bowl, and mix thoroughly. Taste to check the seasoning, and add more yogurt, olive oil, or lemon juice if necessary.

3. Lay the lettuce leaves on their curved sides in a serving dish. Scoop a little of the tuna mixture into each leaf. Finish with a sprinkle of pepper.

Lettuce belongs to the same family as daisies, and people have been eating it in salads for thousands of years.

Growing Onions

Onions can be stored and used throughout the year. They are easy to grow in large pots or straight in the ground and can be grown from seeds. Or you can plant onion sets, which are small onion bulbs that can be purchased at garden centers.

Growing Onions from Sets

1. Use string and pegs to mark out a straight line in the soil. Make a shallow planting trench, using a trowel.

2. Place the onion sets in the trench, making sure the root is at the bottom (the top will be much thinner).

3. Space the onion sets 4 inches apart. You will need about 12 inches between rows.

4. Press the soil back in around the sets so that just the wispy tops are showing. Initially it may be worth covering the sets with netting, because birds often mistake them for worms!

Taking Care of Your Onions

1. Keep the onions watered. Onion patches can become weedy, so be ready to pull up any weeds around your onions.

2. Harvest once the leaves die back and you can see the swollen onions. Use a fork to carefully lift them out of the soil.

3. Dry them out in sunshine until their skins turn papery. One of the easiest ways to store onions is to put them in a net bag and hang them somewhere dry.

4. You could also try making an onion string. Twist each onion around a loop of string with the biggest at the bottom.

Medieval Onions

In medieval times, onions were hung above doorways, as it was believed this would ward off diseases.

Onion Soup

serves
2

2 tablespoons butter

2 tablespoons plus
   1 tablespoon olive oil

5 medium onions, sliced

1 leek, white part only, sliced

1 teaspoon sugar

Salt and pepper

2 beef or vegetable stock cubes

2 cloves garlic, crushed

½ cup red wine

1 small baguette

¾ cup grated cheddar cheese

1. Heat 2 tablespoons of the olive oil and 2 tablespoons of the butter in a large, heavy-bottomed casserole dish. Add the onions, leek, sugar, and salt and pepper, and stir to coat evenly.

2. Cook on the stovetop on low heat, partially covered, stirring occasionally, for 40 to 50 minutes, until the onions are brown and sticky.

3. Dissolve the stock cubes in $4\frac{1}{2}$ cups boiling water.

4. Add the garlic to the cooking onions, turn up the heat, and add the wine. Let this cook for a few minutes, then add the stock.

5. Simmer partially covered for 15 minutes.

6. When you are nearly ready to serve, slice the baguette. Brush the remaining olive oil over both sides of each slice and place on a baking tray. Cover each slice with grated cheese and broil until the cheese is melted.

7. Dish out your soup and pop a few slices of cheesy baguette on top. Enjoy!

Growing Pole Beans

Pole beans are hungry plants that will thrive in the garden or grow in a large pot. Make sure you add some compost or manure. This will ensure that the beans get all the food they need.

Sowing

Pole bean seeds can be planted straight outside. Push them into the ground about ³/₄ inch deep. You can also start them off inside. Follow the instructions on pages 26 to 27. Sow one seed per pot. You'll need six or seven plants. Once they produce their first large leaves, harden them off so they are ready to be planted outside.

Building a Trellis

Some string beans and green beans are not climbing plants, but pole beans are, so before you can plant, you must build them a tepee trellis.

1. You will need seven 5-foot-long bamboo canes and 16 inches of string.

2. Make a rough circle in the soil with your finger, about 3 feet wide.

3. Now push in the canes, evenly spaced around the circle.

4. Get an adult to bunch the canes and tie them together using the string.

Planting

1. Dig a hole next to each cane. Place one plant by each cane.

2. Place your hand over the surface of the pot and turn it upside down—the plant will come away from the pot.

3. Put the plant in a hole and push soil around it to gently firm it in. Water well.

4. Once the beans start to form, they will swell quickly. Start harvesting once the beans reach 8 inches. Any bigger, and they'll taste tough and stringy.

Pests

You can spray some pests off plants using a hose.

Bean and Bacon Spaghetti

----

serves 4

16 ounces spaghetti

2 tablespoons olive oil

14 ounces runner beans, sliced diagonally into ¼ inch pieces

12 slices bacon, chopped

1 tablespoon fresh tarragon, finely chopped

½ cup grated Parmesan cheese

1 egg, beaten

Black pepper

1. Cook the spaghetti in a pot of salted boiling water for 10 minutes, until al dente. Drain it, setting aside a tablespoon of the water the spaghetti was cooked in.

2. Heat the olive oil in a large frying pan. Add the runner beans and cook on medium heat, stirring occasionally for 6 to 8 minutes.

3. Add the bacon and tarragon. Cook until the bacon is browned, and turn off the heat.

4. Add the set-aside cooking water, Parmesan, and egg, and stir quickly for a minute.

5. Add plenty of black pepper and an extra grating of Parmesan before mixing with the pasta and serving.

Runner beans got their name because once they start growing, they run up poles and fences like winding strings.

A few months after planting, give the pods a shake. If you hear the beans rattling inside, they're ready to pick!

Growing Cranberry Beans

Cranberry beans have a beautiful and unusual pattern on their pods. Unlike green beans or garden peas, which are eaten fresh, cranberry beans are usually grown for their dried seeds.

Sowing

Follow the indoor sowing instructions on pages 26 to 27. You'll need five or six pots with one seed in each pot. Keep all seedlings well watered and they will germinate within a few days. Once they have grown their first two leaves, they are ready to be hardened off before planting outside. You can also sow them straight into the ground.

Trellis

1. With the help of an adult, construct a tepee trellis as for the pole beans on page 62.

2. Dig a hole next to each cane. Hold the base of the plant pot in one hand and tap the bottom of the pot to release the plant.

3. Place one plant beside each cane and press the soil firmly in around it.

4. Keep the plants well watered and watch as the beans grow and wind their way around the canes.

Bean Burgers

Did you know that beans, when dried and stored in good conditions, can keep for many years?

makes **4** burgers

1½ pounds fresh cranberry beans, pricked with a fork

1 potato

3 scallions, white parts only, chopped

8 sprigs fresh cilantro, chopped

1 egg

1 teaspoon cumin

1 teaspoon chili flakes

Salt and pepper

Bowl of sesame seeds

1. Preheat the oven to 350°F.

2. Place the cranberry beans in a pan of cold water. Bring to a boil and cook for 20 minutes, until tender.

3. Peel the potato and chop it into four pieces. Place the potato chunks in a pan of cold, salted water. Bring to a boil and cook for 10 minutes.

4. Drain the potatoes and mash them. Add the cranberry beans and mash them into the potatoes.

5. Add the scallions, cilantro, egg, cumin, chili flakes, and salt and pepper. Mix well.

6. Using your hands, divide the mixture into four equal-size pieces. Flatten into burger shapes. It is fine if they feel quite wet. Roll them in the bowl of sesame seeds to coat and place them onto an oven tray covered with foil.

7. Bake for 40 minutes, until nice and golden. Serve in buns with sliced tomato, lettuce, and mayonnaise or the garlic dip (page 84), along with the polenta fries (page 89).

Growing Tomatoes

Tomatoes aren't just red and round—they come in all sorts of shapes, sizes, and colors, from deep purple to orange, yellow, and even stripy green. Whatever type you grow, they're sure to taste delicious!

Sowing

Follow the instructions for sowing seeds indoors on pages 26 to 27. Sow two to three seeds per pot. Once the seeds have germinated, remove the weaker seedlings to leave only one tomato plant per pot. When the plants reach a height of 8 inches, they are ready to be hardened off (see page 29) and planted outside.

Growing Your Tomato Plants

Tomatoes grow best in a warm, sunny environment. If you grow tomatoes outside, it is important that the weather is warm enough. Temperatures need to be above 50°F day and night.

When the weather is warm enough, transfer your plants from their pots to the soil outdoors. They will need around 16 inches of space beside them. They can also be planted in grow bags or larger pots. Once they start to produce fruit, they will need bamboo canes or sticks to support them.

Tomatoes can benefit from an occasional liquid fertilizer feed. This will produce bigger and better tomatoes. Do this every week when the tomato plants start to produce flowers and fruit.

Blight

Blight is a fungal disease that can attack the whole plant. Watch for black patches on stems and leaves. If your tomato plant contracts blight, it's unlikely it will produce a good crop.

Pick the tomatoes when they are bright red.

Tomato, Feta, and Basil Pizza

serves 3

12-ounce puff pastry sheet

2 tablespoons Dijon mustard

2 small tomatoes, sliced

1 tablespoon feta cheese, crumbled

Salt and pepper

Olive oil

Handful of fresh basil leaves

A little milk

1. Preheat the oven to 400°F. Take the puff pastry out of the fridge. Remove the packaging but do not unroll the pastry. Leave it at room temperature for 10 minutes.

2. Unroll the room-temperature pastry on a baking sheet while keeping it on the baking paper provided with it.

3. Roll each edge of the pastry to create a ¼ inch rim around the outside of the tart.

4. Prick the pastry base with a fork to keep the middle from rising in the oven. (You want the edges to rise to create a crust, so don't prick those.)

5. Using the back of a spoon, spread the mustard over the base of the tart. Arrange the tomato slices on top. Sprinkle with the feta, salt, pepper, olive oil, and basil leaves.

6. Using a pastry brush, coat the tart edges with milk. Bake for 12 minutes, until the pastry is crisp and golden.

When tomatoes were first brought to Europe, in the 1700s, people were afraid to eat them because of their bright-red color, which was usually associated with poisonous plants.

Growing Potatoes

The excitement of digging up your own potato crop is hard to beat! Potatoes can be grown straight in the ground, in potato bags, or in large tubs.

Seed Potatoes

Buy seed potatoes in late winter from a garden center or nursery. Place them in an egg carton on a windowsill. They will begin to sprout in a process called chitting, which takes about five weeks. Sprouts need to be about a quarter inch long before the potatoes can be planted outside.

Planting Seed Potatoes Outside

1. Choose a sunny spot to plant your seed potatoes.

2. Using a spade, dig a trench 6 inches deep and 8 inches wide and as long as you have space for. Allow 24 inches between rows.

3. If possible, place some garden compost in the bottom of your trench to help feed the potato plants.

4. Place the seed potatoes in the trench, spacing them 12 inches apart. Cover them with soil. Be careful not to damage the sprouts.

5. Once the potato plants have grown to 8 inches, rake the soil up around the base of each plant. This is called earthing up; it will protect any potatoes growing near the surface and will help support the plant.

6. Keep an eye out for flowers; they are very pretty and are a good sign that your potatoes are almost ready.

7. Use a fork to lift the potatoes and be careful not to poke any! Have a good dig around to make sure you get them all out of the ground.

Potato Blight

Watch out for black patches on leaves and stems. This may be blight and could mean you lose your entire crop! Cut off any infected leaves and dig up any potatoes before blight spreads to the whole plant.

Potato Pancakes

serves **4**

4 medium potatoes, peeled and chopped into small chunks

6 tablespoons finely grated Parmesan cheese

4 tablespoons flour

2 eggs

Salt and pepper

1 tablespoon butter

2 tablespoons sunflower oil

Optional: 4 fried eggs

1. Place the potatoes in a pan of cold, salted water and bring to a boil. Simmer for 10 minutes, until tender.

2. Drain the potatoes and mash them.

3. Add the Parmesan, flour, eggs, and salt and pepper, and mix well.

4. Heat the butter and sunflower oil in a frying pan.

5. When the butter has melted, add three or four (depending on the size of your pan) tablespoon-size dollops of the potato mix. Flatten them using a spatula (you want the cakes to be fairly thin). Cook for 2 to 3 minutes, until golden. Flip them over and cook for the same amount of time on the other side.

6. Once the first batch is done, add a little more sunflower oil or butter to the pan, and cook the next batch. Continue until you have used all the mix.

7. Serve the potato pancakes with fried eggs for a yummy breakfast or lunchtime treat.

Potatoes are one of the most complete vegetables to be found in terms of vitamin, protein, and mineral content.

Watch out for birds that want to eat your spinach. If birds are a problem, cover your crop with netting.

Growing Spinach

Spinach leaves are tasty and good for you. Young leaves are perfect for a salad or can be gently steamed. Spinach grows best in cooler temperatures. It grows quickly and can be cut again and again.

Sow new rows every two to three weeks and you'll have a continuous supply.

How to Grow

1. Mark out a row with a string line. Leave 12 inches between rows.

2. Using your fingers or a trowel, make a trench about 1 inch deep.

3. Carefully place a seed every 1 to 1½ inches.

4. Gently cover the seeds with soil and water.

5. Leaves will appear in two to three weeks. They are ready to pick once five or six of the larger leaves have appeared. New leaves will appear and you'll be able to pick the leaves two or three times before the crop will finish.

Spinach Omelette

1 pound spinach leaves
2 tablespoons pine nuts
2 tablespoons olive oil
1 medium onion, finely chopped
Salt and pepper
¼ teaspoon grated nutmeg
8 eggs, beaten

1. Preheat the oven to 350°F.

2. Lightly toast the pine nuts in a large ovenproof nonstick frying pan on medium heat. When most have turned golden, remove them from the pan and set them aside.

3. Heat one tablespoon of the olive oil in the frying pan, then add the onion and cook for 2 minutes, until translucent and soft.

4. Gradually add the spinach, using tongs to lift and toss it until wilted. Season with the salt, pepper, and nutmeg. If there is more than a teaspoon of excess moisture in the pan, drain it off using a spoon.

5. Drizzle the remaining tablespoon of olive oil around the spinach in the pan and increase the heat. Pour the eggs over the spinach and cook for 2 minutes, until the eggs have set at the bottom and are still a little wobbly at the top. Use a spatula to lift the spinach and let the egg run underneath.

6. Spread the toasted pine nuts over the top of the omelette, and finish in the oven for a couple of minutes until the top of the omelette has set.

Growing Garlic

This rather smelly vegetable is used in many different recipes in the kitchen. It can be dried and stored so you can use it all year round!

Planting Garlic

1. It is best to buy garlic bulbs from a garden center to ensure that they're healthy and free from disease. Separate the individual garlic cloves from the bulb.

2. Using a string line, mark out a straight line.

3. Use your finger to push each clove 2 inches into the soil. The clove should have the wide root part facing down. Leave 6 inches of space between each clove and 12 inches between rows.

4. In a few weeks, small green shoots will emerge.

5. When the leaves start to turn yellow, use a fork to gently lift the bulbs out of the soil.

Rusty Garlic

Watch out for rust, orangey-brown spots that may appear on leaves. There isn't much you can do about rust. If it gets too bad and covers the whole plant, you can dig up the garlic early. It will be smaller, but leave it to dry and you can still eat it.

Garlic Dip with Crudités

1 large garlic bulb, unpeeled

1 cup Greek yogurt

1 teaspoon ground cumin

Salt and pepper

Juice of ½ lemon

An assortment of vegetables
for dipping, such as:

  Carrots

  Celery

  Endives

  Cauliflower

  Red pepper

  Radishes

1. Preheat the oven to 280°F. Bake the garlic bulb on a baking sheet for 1 hour.

2. Cool the baked garlic for 5 minutes. Then separate the cloves from the bulb and gently squeeze the cooked flesh out of the skins into a bowl.

3. Using a teaspoon or fork, mash the garlic flesh until it is smooth. Add the yogurt, cumin, salt and pepper, and lemon juice, and mix.

4. Peel the carrots, and de-seed the peppers. Then chop all your dipping vegetables (known as crudités) into sticks or bite-size chunks.

5. Place the bowl of dip on a large serving plate, and arrange the vegetables around the bowl for dunking.

Garlic has many scientifically proven medicinal properties, from anti-bacterial to antiworm and antiviral!

Growing Zucchini

Zucchini belongs to the same family as cucumbers, squash, and pumpkins. Just one or two plants will give you enough zucchini to last through the growing season!

Growing Zucchini

1. Start seeds off indoors. Sow one seed each into three or four pots to ensure that you get at least two healthy plants.

2. Zucchini seeds can also be sown straight into the ground. Sow seeds 1 inch deep and leave at least 16 inches of space between plants.

Planting Outside

1. If you started growing your plants indoors, harden the plants off (see page 29) once they have produced four to six leaves.

2. Dig a hole, using a trowel or spade, and plant. Make sure the soil isn't piled too close to the stem, as this can cause it to rot.

3. Make a ring of soil around the plant. This will keep water from running off and make sure it goes right down to the roots.

4. Zucchini are thirsty plants, so keep them well watered.

Harvesting

Be sure to harvest your zucchini when they are young and sweet (around 4 to 8 inches). They grow so fast that they can quickly become too big. Check them every day.

Flower Food

Did you know that zucchini flowers can also be eaten? Deep-fry them in batter for a delicious snack!

Zucchini and Polenta Fries

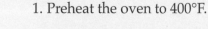

serves 4

4 medium zucchini

4 ounces polenta

1 cup grated Parmesan cheese

1 sprig rosemary

¾ cup sunflower oil

1. Preheat the oven to 400°F.

2. Chop the zucchini into roughly 3-inch by ½-inch sticks.

3. Put the polenta and Parmesan in a bowl.

4. Strip the leaves off the sprig of rosemary and finely chop. Add to the bowl of Parmesan and polenta, and mix together.

5. Place the sunflower oil in a bowl. Dip each zucchini stick in the oil, then roll it in the polenta mix until coated.

6. Bake the fries on a baking sheet for 25 minutes, until golden.

Beware the giant in the garden! If left, zucchini can grow to about 3 feet long.

Growing Swiss Chard

Swiss chard is an amazing plant! It grows quickly, can be picked continuously, and will survive well in the cold. It's also very tasty! Swiss chard comes in an array of colors, from green, white, and pink to deep reds and yellow. Growing chard will bring a splash of color to your garden.

How to Grow

Swiss chard can be sown directly into the ground in the same way as beets (see page 99). You can also sow chard seeds indoors. Sow two or three seeds into each pot.

When the seedlings have two to three leaves, it's time to plant them outside. Remember to harden them off first (see page 29). Dig a hole in the soil, put one plant in, and surround it with soil. The farther apart you plant your seedlings, the bigger they will get.

Swiss chard is one of the most nutritious vegetables you can eat. It contains a high amount of vitamin K, which is important for helping wounds to heal.

Swiss chard grows quickly. After just a few weeks, you can start picking it. Cut the stems near the base of the plant. Leave the very smallest leaves, as these will be your next harvest!

Chard-Noodle Stir-Fry

serves
4

1 pound Swiss chard

2 teaspoons sesame oil

1 onion, chopped

2 cloves garlic, finely sliced

1 thumb-size piece of ginger,
finely sliced

2 portions of straight-to-wok
noodles

Drizzle of soy sauce

5 scallions, white parts only,
finely chopped

½ lime

Sesame seeds

1. Slice the stalk ends of the chard into little chunks and the leafy ends into strips.

2. Heat the sesame oil in a wok (or a very large, deep-sided pan) and add the chopped stalk ends and onion. Soften for 2 minutes, stirring frequently. Then add the garlic and ginger.

3. After 30 seconds, add the noodles and soy sauce. Use a wooden spoon or tongs to separate the noodle strands. Cook for 2 to 3 minutes, stirring constantly.

4. Add the sliced chard leaves and, stirring constantly, cook for 1 to 2 minutes, until softened.

5. Add the scallions, and toss for 30 seconds.

6. Serve with a squeeze of lime juice and a sprinkle of sesame seeds. Eat immediately.

Growing Eggplant

Eggplants come from the same family as tomatoes and potatoes. They thrive in hot and humid conditions, so it's best to start them indoors, then plant them outside once the weather is warm enough.

Sowing Eggplant Seeds Indoors

1. Eggplants take a long time to reach their full size.

2. Sow 2 to 3 seeds into 3½-inch-wide pots.

3. Water them and place somewhere warm. Most windowsills will be fine for this.

4. After about three weeks, the seeds will start to germinate. Remove the weaker seedlings, leaving one strong plant in each pot.

5. Once the plants reach around 8 inches, their roots will begin to run out of space in the small pots. Transfer them to larger pots or plant them outside, hardening them off first (see page 29).

Planting Outside

It is best to plant your eggplants outside when both the days and nights are warm.

WATER & WATCH IT GROW!

1. Dig holes big enough for each plant.

2. Put a plant in each hole and firm the soil around it. Leave at least 24 inches between each plant.

3. Water well. In three or four weeks, you will see flowers begin to develop. From these flowers, your eggplants will grow!

Eggplant

Eggplants can be black, purple, or white.

Eggplant Rounds with Tomato Topping

serves 4

3 eggplants

2 to 3 tablespoons plus 1 tablespoon olive oil

½ cup Greek yogurt

1 lime

½ clove garlic, crushed

Salt and pepper

10 ounces cherry tomatoes, quartered

6 sprigs of cilantro, chopped

1. Preheat the oven to 350°F.

2. Slice the eggplants width-wise into ½-inch-thick rounds.

3. Place the 2 to 3 tablespoons of olive oil in a small bowl, then, using a pastry brush, cover both sides of each round with olive oil.

4. Bake the eggplant for 30 minutes, until golden. Halfway through cooking, turn them over to cook both sides evenly.

5. Meanwhile, place the yogurt in a bowl and add the juice of half the lime. Add the garlic and a pinch of salt and pepper. Taste to check the seasoning.

6. Place the tomatoes in a bowl and drizzle them with the remaining olive oil and a squeeze of juice from the remaining lime half.

7. Arrange the cooked eggplant on a serving plate and dollop with the yogurt, then the tomatoes, then the cilantro. Enjoy!

Beets can be purple, white, or yellow.

Growing Beets

Beets are one of the easiest vegetables to grow in the garden. Not only do we eat the root part of the plant, but the young leaves are also delicious.

Sowing Beets

1. Make a trench about ½ inch deep.

2. Place the beet seeds individually into the trench, about 1 to 1½ inches apart.

3. Cover the seeds with soil and water them. Keep the ground moist as the beets grow.

4. When the seedlings emerge, it is important to give them enough space to grow to a good size. Each beet plant will need around 4 to 6 inches of space. Choose which ones you want to keep, and remove the other seedlings.

5. Harvest your beets when they are the size of golf balls.

Chocolate Beet Cake

serves **8**

4 ounces unsweetened chocolate
1 large beet
¾ cup butter, at room temperature
1 cup sugar
3 eggs
1 cup flour
¾ cup cocoa powder
1 teaspoon vanilla extract
1 tablespoon maple syrup or honey
Pinch of salt

1. Preheat the oven to 350°F.

2. Grease a loaf pan with butter, then line it with parchment paper.

3. Break the chocolate into small pieces and place it in a heat-proof bowl. Place the bowl over a small saucepan of simmering water on the stovetop. Make sure the bottom of the bowl doesn't touch the water. Let the chocolate slowly melt.

4. Wash the beets and trim off any scraggly bits. Using a cheese grater, grate the whole beet, skin included. Wash your hands to prevent them from staining red.

5. Beat the butter and sugar in a mixing bowl, stirring quickly until creamy. Add the eggs and beat to blend. Gently stir in the flour, cocoa powder, vanilla, maple syrup or honey, salt, melted chocolate, and the beet, until everything is combined.

6. Transfer the batter into the prepared loaf pan.

7. Bake for 1 hour.

8. Let the cake cool for 5 minutes, then gently remove it from the pan, and leave it to cool on a rack.

It is a good idea to wear an apron when cooking with beets, as they contain the pigment betalain, which can be used to dye fabric!

Growing Chili Peppers

Chili peppers have a hot and spicy flavor. They do best on a warm windowsill or a sunny spot in the garden.

Sowing Chili Peppers

1. Chili peppers need a long growing time before they produce fruit, so sow seeds early. Sow three to four seeds in each pot.

2. Place the pots somewhere warm, such as a well-heated room. The seeds need lots of heat and moisture.

3. In two to three weeks, the seeds will begin to germinate. Use a pencil to help you carefully remove the weaker seedlings in the pot, leaving just the strongest.

4. Move the pots into a space where they will get lots of light.

Growing Chili Pepper Plants

1. Once the chili pepper plants reach a height of 8 inches, move them into a bigger pot or plant them outside in a warm, sunny spot when all risk of frost has passed.

2. Leave at least 16 inches between each plant.

3. Water regularly, especially when the weather is hot.

Consider growing a mild type of chili (see varieties on page 106). Some types can be very hot and irritate your skin. If you choose to grow a hot variety, it's a good idea to wear gloves when handling the peppers.

Mexican Spice

Did you know that chili peppers originally come from Mexico?

Chili-Pepper Hot Chocolate

Did you know that chili peppers contain five times more vitamin C than oranges?

serves
2

2½ cups skim milk

1 chili pepper

2 tablespoons cocoa

1 pinch of cinnamon

2 teaspoons sugar

1. Heat the milk in a small saucepan on low heat.

2. Using a sharp knife, make a little cut lengthwise in the chili pepper. If you want only a little hint of spice, make a smaller cut.

3. Place the pepper in the milk pan. The spice will infuse the milk. Wash your hands thoroughly. Chili peppers can sting if they get near your eyes.

4. When you see little milk bubbles at the edge of the pan, add the cocoa and cinnamon. Use a wooden spoon or whisk to stir.

5. Add the sugar to the pan and stir well. Check whether you are happy with the taste. If it's not spicy enough, leave it to infuse for a bit longer.

6. When you're happy with the taste, place a tea strainer over a mug and carefully pour in the hot chocolate. The strainer will catch the chili pepper. Wait a few minutes for the drink to cool. Enjoy!

Further Information

Growing Varieties

Beets: Detroit Dark Red beets are a classic red beet. You could also try Golden beets, a deep-yellow beet that tastes great when roasted. Chioggia beets are sweet and have a wonderful striped pattern within.

Carrots: For a tasty, fast-growing carrot, try Nantes. Chantenay are small carrots great for growing in pots. For something totally different, try Purple Sun.

Chili Peppers: Padrón chili peppers are mild and delicious grilled. Cayenne Sweet is another mild variety.

Cranberry Beans: For a striking bean worth having in any vegetable plot, Tongue of Fire shelling beans are hard to beat.

Eggplant: Japanese eggplant will grow better outside than some other varieties and can produce plenty of flavorsome deep-purple fruits.

Garlic: Purple Stripe garlic produces purple-tinged garlic bulbs. Or you could grow the enormous but milder-tasting Elephant garlic.

Kale: Tuscan Black Palm kale produces upright dark green leaves—delicious!

Lettuce: Crisp and sweet Little Gem is the perfect lettuce. Alternatively the spotted Freckles romaine lettuce will give color to a salad bowl.

Onions: Try the traditional white Stuttgart giant onion, which stores well in the cold months, or the dark crimson Red Baron onion.

Peas: For a fast crop of peas, give Maestro peas a try.

Potatoes: You can buy first earlies, second earlies, or main crop potatoes. First earlies are the quickest to mature and take around 100 days from planting until harvest. Try Dark Red Norland, a lovely red potato, perfect for any use in the kitchen.

Runner Beans: Scarlet Emperor beans produce an abundance of tasty long beans. Keep picking and they will keep growing!

Spinach: Bloomsdale and Palco are spinach types that are quick to grow and can be picked time and time again. Perpetual spinach will grow well into the cold months.

Swiss Chard: Bright Lights swiss chard will give a splash of color to your garden in yellow, pink, and white stems.

Tomatoes: Red Alert bush tomatoes are perfect for growing in pots. They produce masses of sweet fruit long before most other varieties.

Zucchini: Yellow and green varieties are available. You could also plant round types, such as Ronde de Nice, which are harvested when they are the size of tennis balls.

Supplies

Seeds, small vegetable plants, and gardening equipment can be brought from most local garden centers or nurseries. For a wider choice try buying online.

Glossary

aphid: a small insect that eats by sucking the juices of plants

blight: a plant disease that destroys parts or all of a plant

bulb: the rounded part of a plant that begins to grow below ground

clay: a thick, heavy soil

decompose: to rot and break down

diet: the food or drink usually consumed by a person or animal

fertilization: the successful coming together of male and female cells

fertilizer: natural materials such as manure and food scraps, that contain nitrogen and are spread on soil to support plant growth

flower: the part of a plant that has petals and makes fruit and seeds

fruit: the part of a plant that holds the seeds

fungi: organisms that help to decompose dead plants and animals

garden compost: made up of garden and kitchen waste, compost is added to soil to fertilize plants

germination: the process when a seed begins to sprout and grow

harden off: to put plants outside for a few hours each day to get them used to colder temperatures before they are planted outside permanently

leaves: the parts of a plant that absorb energy from the sun to help them photosynthesize

mildew: a powdery fungus that grows on plants

nectar: a sweet liquid produced by a plant that attracts insects

nutrient: something that helps people, plants, and animals live and grow

organic material: dead and rotting leaves, plants, and wood found in soils

pod: the long, thin pouch that contains seeds of a plant such as a pea or bean

pollen: tiny yellow powder made by a flowering plant

pollination: the spread of pollen from one flower to another, to allow fertilization

root: the part of the plant that usually grows underground

sap: the liquid that carries nutrients and water to all parts of a plant

seed: the small part of a flowering plant that can grow into a new plant

shoot: the new growth of a plant

soil: the top layer of earth in which plants grow

soil bacteria: tiny single-celled creatures that can help to break down decaying organic material in soil

stamen: the male part of the flower

stem: the main structure of a plant that supports the leaves, flowers, and fruit

stigma: the female part of the flower that receives pollen

thin out: to remove weak seedlings from a pot or soil to ensure that strong seedlings have enough space to grow

Index

Acknowledgments

Thank you to the following for their help with this book:
Susan Allen, Tom and Josh Martin, Isabella and Mia McGregor, Lily and Polly Munson, Cerys and Liam O'Sullivan, Zachary Pang, Ruth Thomas, and Olivia Walker.

Photography Credits

The publishers would like to thank the following for their permission to reproduce photographs:
Kew planting photography by Thom Hudson © Kew Gardens, except for: 8 top, 43 middle, 47 bottom, 55 bottom, 59 top, 71 top, 74 bottom, 75 top, 94 bottom, 95 middle and bottom, 99 bottom by Joe Archer © The Board of Trustees of the Royal Botanic Gardens, Kew 2016.

Recipe photography by Ian Garlick © Wayland 2016.

All remaining photographs © Shutterstock: 8 bottom left by Africa Studio; 8 bottom right by C Levers; 9 top by Norman Chan; 9 middle left by Pixeljoy; 9 bottom by Kostiantyn Kravchenko; 11 top by Peter Baumann; 11 bottom by Bogdan Wankowicz; 12 top by showcake; 12 (bumblebee) by hsagencia; 12 bottom by TippaPatt; 12 and 13 middle (honeybee) by Peter Waters; 13 bottom left by Sergej Razvodovskij; 13 bottom right by Bahadir Yeniceri; 18 left by Bernatskaya Oxana; 18 middle and 19 top (woodlice) by Gerald A. DeBoer; 19 middle by Evan Lorne; 19 bottom by Marina Lohrbach; 20 middle by johnbraid; 22 by fresher; 32 top (centipede) by Boonroong; 32 and 35 (ladybugs) by StevenRusselSmithPhotos; 34 top right (garden snail) by Jiri Hera; 34 top left (caterpillars) by Sarah2; 34 middle by Alexander Raths; 34 bottom by TwilightArtPictures; 35 top by dabjola; 35 middle by Vadym Zaitsez; 35 bottom by Julie Vader; 36 bottom by kazoka; 38 by Antonio Danna; 50 top by oksana2010; 55 top by Dieter Hawlan; 55 middle by rodimov; 71 middle by Anna North; 74 top by Swellphotography; 79 top by Nataliia Melnychuk; 86 top by EagleEyes; 90 top by Kanjanee Chaisin; 90 bottom by Arena Photo UK; 94 top by Nataliia Melnychuk; 95 left by Sarin Kunthong.